CITY OF GLOUCESTER

FRONT COVER: *St Mary's Square. Monument by Edward W. Thornhill of Dublin, erected 1862, to Bishop Hooper burnt here in 1555. Behind is St Mary's Gate, the great gate of the abbey, through which came its means of livelihood; it has Transitional Norman vaulting and a 13th-century arch; iron gates, 18th century, from Nuremberg.*

ABOVE: *Gloucester from the air, looking towards the north-west. The city is dominated by the cathedral.*

CITY OF GLOUCESTER

Gilbert Thurlow, Dean of Gloucester

'WHERE'ER WE TREAD, 'tis haunted, holy ground' says Byron's Childe Harold, travelling in Greece and in his mind's eye seeing the people, tribes and nations who through the ages have shaped the landscape and left their traces behind them. We can do the same in Gloucester and in its hills and vale and river. It is an effort worth making, for so much is hidden beneath and behind man's modern works. We can see in imagination the Roman city of Glevum, at the height of its splendour, bearing a modest resemblance to those Roman frontier cities which suffered gradual decay rather than centuries of destruction and rebuilding. Go to Timgad in Algeria or Jerash in Jordan, outposts of the Roman Empire; note the simplicity and efficiency of their city planning, with walls enclosing a rectagular area divided by main streets running north to south and east to west, dignified with colonnades behind which are luxurious houses and small shops. Near the city centre is the forum or open market and the basilica or aisled public hall, and here and there a theatre or amphitheatre. When Christian churches began to dominate the Roman scene, they continued with the forum and basilica arrangement so that when, centuries later, the Normans rebuilt Gloucester Abbey – now the cathedral – its aisled nave resembled in shape and size, if not location, the basilica built and destroyed here long before, whilst its cloister similarly recalled the forum.

Long before the Romans came, men were living on the surrounding hills. Churchdown Hill, three miles east of Gloucester Cathedral, has Iron Age fortifications, and pottery of the period was found here, while along the escarpment of the Cotswold Hills, four to six miles east of Gloucester, are earth works of similar date on Crickley Hill,

★

LEFT: *The Birdlip mirror, in the City Museum, Brunswick Road. Early Iron Age* c. AD 25, *its overall height is 15¼ inches. Three types of engraving tools were used to create the perfectly represented Celtic scroll patterns, and the bronze handle parts were probably cast by the lost wax method.*

FACING PAGE: *The Roman East Gate, excavated 1979-80, and enclosed in a gigantic 'glass case', revealing work of several periods from that of the Romans onwards.*

Painswick Hill, and elsewhere. The Celts were the most artistic of the restless peoples who were expanding around Europe; they came to Britain, Italy, Greece and Asia Minor (where St Paul wrote them a letter 'to the Galatians'). Of all the brilliant examples of geometrically ornamented bronze work they have left us, one of the most striking is the mirror ornamented with curving scroll patterns found in a grave at Barrow Wake between Crickley Hill and Birdlip (on the Roman road to Cirencester) and now in Gloucester Museum.

The history of Gloucester began when Claudius was Emperor of Rome (AD 41-54). He extended Roman influence in Britain, first through friendly local chieftains, then in AD 43 with an invasion by four legions, two of which were to remain in Britain until the end of Roman rule. The invading army was commanded by Aulus Plautius, one of whose officers, Vespasian (later to become Emperor in 69) subdued much of the West Country. Under Ostorius Scapula, Plautius' successor, the Fosse Way, stretching virtually straight from Exeter through Cirencester to Lincoln, formed the Roman Empire's western frontier, and forces were planted on it in AD 47 to keep out the Welsh tribes. From it Ostorius pushed along the line of the Ermin Way north-west to the river Severn; here the 20th legion was sent from Colchester in 49, and Glevum, a legionary fortress 43 acres in extent was built as a base from which Ostorius attacked the Silures in South Wales. Their leader, Caractacus (Caradoc) was captured in AD 51 and sent to Rome, where his dignified plea for freedom has become one of the great sayings of history.

Vespasian became emperor in AD 69. Among the generals he sent to England was Frontinus, who arrived in 74. Frontinus conquered the Silures, and the legionary base was moved westward from Gloucester to Caerleon. Gloucester retained its importance, however, as the nearest place to the sea where the Severn could be conveniently crossed, and under Emperor Nerva there was founded here in AD 96 to 98 a chartered town for the settlement of veterans, Colonia Nerva Glevensium. There were only four such settlements in Britain, the others being Colchester, Lincoln and York.

Much excavation of Roman Gloucester, and of the royal palace at Kingsholm nearby, has been carried out in recent years, largely in connection with modern building works. Valuable finds include a medieval tower and the remains of the Roman East Gate in Eastgate Street, a Roman column now in Gloucester Museum, a drainage system at the Cross, and parts of ramparts, walls, gateways, towers, mosaic floors and painted plaster walls. The forum appears to have extended to about 100 metres south from St Michael's Tower at the Cross, and to have been about 72 metres from east to west, while the basilica (which appears to have been roughly the size of the present cathedral nave) lay east and west to the south of the forum, interrupting the Roman predecessor of Southgate Street. The Roman wall, completed about 300 AD protected the city thereafter for 1,000 years.

The 'long sunset' of Rome's decline was gradual in Gloucestershire, and Saxon infiltration into the area seems to have resulted in the re-use of building materials rather than deliberate destruction of Roman Gloucester. Christianity may well have come to Gloucester by 200 AD, by which date it was certainly in Britain, and while the conquering Saxons subdued it here for a time, it survived in Ireland and in remote parts of western Wales and Scotland. The Saxons captured Gloucester in 577 following the battle of Dyrham and did much damage, and thereafter the Saxon kingdom of Mercia which included Gloucester remained heathen until the accession of the Christian King Wulphere in 657. Wulphere appears to have planned to found a religious house in Gloucester, and his successor Ethelred to have carried the plan forward.

In 681 King Ethelred gave the town of Gloucester to Prince Osric, one of his ministers or viceroys, and under Osric the religious foundation began its life. 681 is perhaps the most significant date in Gloucester's long history, for Gloucester Abbey, now the cathedral, became and long remained a meeting place of royal and national importance. Shortly before 681 events of crucial importance for England had been taking place. At the Synod of Whitby in 664 the English Church had agreed to unite with the Church of western Europe, and to cease being an outpost of Celtic Christianity. In 669 a dynamic old Greek monk, Theodore, had become Archbishop of Canterbury and in a few years had reorganized the English Church on a firm and lasting foundation. At the Synod of Hertford in 673, many of the rules by which the Church has since lived were drawn up, and at the Council of Hatfield in 680, the Church had attested its unity with the rest of Christendom – showing an outlook which modern advocates of the United Nations are still struggling to realize. Archbishop Theodore himself came to Gloucester and dedicated the new convent to St Peter the Apostle, as a double foundation for monks and nuns. Its first abbess was Kyneburga, Osric's sister.

She was succeeded in 710 by Eadburga, widowed queen of Wulphere. With the death of Eva, the third abbess (735-767), the convent's life was interrupted by wars between the Saxon kingdoms. It was re-founded in 823 by Beornwulf, King of Mercia, with secular priests, who in turn were replaced by King Canute with Benedictine monks. In 1058, after destruction by fire, it was again re-founded, by Aldred, Bishop of Worcester.

In 909 another significant event in Gloucester's history took place. The body of St Oswald, King of Northumbria (who had been slain by Penda at Maserfield in 641) was brought from its burial place at Bardney in Lincolnshire to Gloucester. St Oswald's Priory was built to hallow his memory and to house his tomb, which became a saintly shrine in 1113. St Oswald's was founded by Aethelred, ruler of Mercia under Alfred the Great, and Aethel-

fleda his queen – Alfred's daughter and a staunch warrior against Danish raiders. The priory, whose ruins (on the site of the Roman municipal tile works) have recently been excavated, stood north-west of the Roman city and close to the royal palace of Kingsholm and near the Roman and Saxon quays by a branch of the river Severn. Not far away is the parish church of St Mary de Lode, i.e. 'of the river crossing'. The excavations reveal that the priory church possessed a western apse, a familiar feature of Carolingian churches such as those at Bamberg, Mainz and elsewhere. Close by were discovered the remains of a small furnace and moulds showing where the church's 10th-century bells were cast (as in the Saxon Winchester Cathedral).

10th-century Gloucester with its royal palace, its men-at-arms who helped defeat a Danish force in 914, its status as the burial place of Aethel-

red in 911 and of Aethelfleda in 918, was clearly the central city of the Mercian kingdom. Yet the coins minted here were minted by the kings of England: by Alfred the Great from 884 to 899, by Aethelstan from 924 to 939 and by later kings from Edgar to Henry III during the years 959 to 1272. However, Gloucester was not destined to develop as England's royal centre. Winchester, capital of Wessex, had always been more important, and under the brief Danish rule begun by Canute in 1016, followed by the Norman Conquest in 1066, London became and has remained England's capital.

The Normans

Edward the Confessor, King of England from 1042 to 1066, 'was at heart not an English king but a French monk', enthusiastic not so much for ruling England but rather for the life

4

FACING PAGE: *St Oswald's Priory. North wall of nave; left, two arches of about 1230, blocked about 1540. Right, four Romanesque arches of about 1120, inserted in a Saxon wall of about 890. At the Dissolution the north aisle became a parish church, St Catherine's, eventually replaced by the 20th-century church of St Catherine's, a mile to the east.*

*

ABOVE: *Westgate Street. St Nicholas Church (left) has a conspicuous and splendid tower, with multiple windows, fine buttresses and parapets. The leaning spire was shortened in 1783 and given its charmingly pinnacled summit. St Nicholas House (right of church) is timber framed, with a fine 18th-century street front of brick and stone with a pediment flanked by balustrading. The cathedral tower overlooks all.*

*

RIGHT: *St Mary de Crypt Church, Southgate Street. Largely rebuilt in the 15th century, with tall slender tower, but since 1908 sadly lacking its pinnacles.*

of the Norman clergy with whom he had long lived. He brought Normans into leading positions in Church and State, with their superiority over the Anglo-Saxons in manners, culture and art. In 1055 he founded England's first great Norman church, Westminster Abbey. It was consecrated in 1065, and there Aldred, Archbishop of York, crowned William the Conqueror King of England on Christmas Day, 1066. The Norman leaders, Scandinavian in origin, retained all their Viking energy in war and colonization, but had become converts to Latin culture, with its instinct for political unity and administrative organization and consolidation. They had a deep devotion to Holy Church and a deep respect for the learning of the clergy, who alone could provide them with the adminis-

trators they needed. These facts explain the almost miraculous speed with which England was revolutionized following the battle of Hastings. In Gloucester their outstanding achievement was the replacement of Aldred's St Peter's Abbey, begun only 39 years before, by a vast new one begun in 1089 by the Norman abbot, Serlo (described in detail in *Gloucester Cathedral* by Seiriol Evans in the Pitkin series). As to other Norman work in Gloucester, at St Oswald's Priory there survives an arcade of arches on piers with scalloped capitals. There is also Norman work in the parish churches of St Mary de Crypt and St Nicholas where there is a fine tympanum showing an *Agnus Dei*, and columns and arches inside; there is the western arch of the central tower of St Mary de

Lode and a Norman doorway in St Mary Magdalene, London Road; and St Mary's Gate in College Green has three fine bays of ribbed 'transitional' Norman vaulting. Llanthony Priory, off the Hempsted Road, begun in 1136, was a refuge for the monks of the Norman Augustinian Llanthony Priory founded in 1109 among the hostile people of the Vale of Ewyas in Monmouthshire. The site of the Norman Gloucester Castle is now occupied by H M Prison.

Of the Normans buried in Gloucester, probably the most attractive although least effective as a ruler was Robert Curthose, the Conqueror's eldest son. As ruler of Normandy he was inept. He was equally hopeless at supporting a rebellion intended to set him on the English throne in place of his brother Rufus. In 1087 both came face to face in Gloucester where as a result of the intrigues, a fire destroyed much of the city. A second rebellion, this time against his younger brother the new King Henry I, led to the battle of Tinchebrai in 1106, where Robert was defeated. He was imprisoned at Wareham, Devizes, Bristol and finally at Cardiff Castle where he died in 1134. His effigy is before the cathedral high altar, and an inscription in the Chapter House reads: *Hic Jacet Robertus Curtus* (here lies Robert Curthose).

Domesday Book

The 'Laud' Chronicle, written at Peterborough in 1154, and now in the Bodleian Library, Oxford, tells us under the year 1085: 'The King [William the Conqueror] spent Christmas with his Counsellors at Gloucester, and held his court there for five days, which was followed by a three-day synod held by the Archbishop and clergy . . . After this the King had important

*

LEFT: *St Mary de Crypt Church. Elegant tall pillars and arches. Fine ashlar walling, and faded wall paintings. Perpendicular stone chapel screens. Robert Raikes' desk and 19th-century profile.*

FACING PAGE, LEFT: *King Edward's Tower, the remains of the gatehouse admitting from Westgate Street to the cathedral, and built by Edward I.*

FACING PAGE, RIGHT: *St Michael's Tower at Gloucester Cross, now a museum. The rest of the church was demolished in 1956. Its window has glass of 1878.*

deliberations and exhaustive discussions with his Council about this land and how it was peopled, and with what sort of men. Then he sent his men all over England into every Shire to ascertain how many hundreds of "hides" of land there were in each Shire, and how much land and livestock the King himself owned in the country, and what annual dues were lawfully his from each Shire. He also had it recorded how much land his Archbishops had and his Diocesan Bishops, his Abbots and his Earls, and what or how much each man who was a landholder had in land or in livestock, and how much money it was worth. So very thoroughly did he have the enquiry carried out that there was not a single "hide", not one virgate of land, not even one ox, nor one cow, nor one pig which escaped notice in his survey.'

This urgent task was carried out to enable disputes over ownership to be justly settled, and for preparations for national defence to be adequately made and paid for, and also to satisfy the king's greed for wealth. The commissioners for the *descriptio* or survey of Gloucestershire probably sat at Gloucester, Bristol, Winchcombe, Cirencester and in the Forest of Dean; 'the men of the Shire' testified before them as to details of ownership, and jurors confirmed the testimonies. The Gloucester survey tells of payments in money (£36), honey and Forest of Dean iron for making nails, etc. Payments were also received from the mint and from houses. Evidence from this survey, and also from the Evesham survey of 1100, suggests a lively city with a population of about 3,000 and already with a strong civic sense. The castle symbolized royal power. Its original motte and bailey were soon extended and dominated by a great tower, and presumably the whole was integrated with the old Roman city walls. The sheriff of Gloucester was by hereditary right the castellan. There was a close link between the castle and St Peter's Abbey and, intermittently, with Llanthony Abbey also. Domesday illustrates the brilliant leadership of the new Norman Abbot of St Peter's, Serlo. In a few years he built up the abbey estates and their productivity, as well as raising its spiritual life and the number of its monks, its reputation and its economic condition, to a far higher degree than ever before, and all the while building the vast new abbey church.

Royalty and Gloucester

Royal occasions in medieval Gloucester punctuate its history like political lightning flashes in a stormy age. Its accessibility by river and road from all directions, its strategic importance and value, the hunting in the Forest of Dean and the hospitality of St Peter's, St Oswald's and the castle, combined to make it an attractive place for royal activities. The interest of the kings of Mercia and their successors in St Peter's, St Oswald's and Kingsholm Palace has already been mentioned. Edward the Confessor held a council

here on 8 September 1051. That year he began a custom which his successors followed; in the words of the Anglo-Saxon Chronicle: 'William I kept great state. He wore his royal crown three times a year when in England: at Easter in Winchester, at Whitsuntide in Westminster, at Christmas in Gloucester. Then all the great men of England were assembled about him . . .' In 1063 Edward was in Gloucester receiving the head of Griffith, Prince of the Welsh, defeated by Harold.

In 1093 King Rufus, taken ill at Gloucester and fearing death, vowed many things to God. He filled the see of Canterbury, vacant five years, by appointing as archbishop the Abbot of Bec, Anselm, who was consecrated in Gloucester Abbey. In 1123 Henry I held a council at Gloucester, at which William de Corbeuil was elected Archbishop of Canterbury. Henry I died in 1135. His daughter Matilda, widow of the Holy Roman Emperor and the obvious successor to the English throne, was abroad. In her absence Stephen, a grandson of William I, snatched it. Robert of Gloucester, illegitimate son of Henry I, invited Matilda to Gloucester in 1139 to claim the throne and usurp Stephen. But their efforts were unsuccessful and in 1147 Robert died. In 1154 Stephen also died. A miserable period of civil war ended and Matilda's son by her second husband, Geoffrey Plantagenet, became King of England and of half of France as Henry II.

The next royal event of significance in Gloucester was on 28 October 1216, when there took place in St Peter's Abbey the only coronation of an English monarch outside Westminster Abbey since the Conquest. Despite the sealing of *Magna Carta* in 1215, civil war prevailed between John and the barons, who had offered the crown to Prince Louis of France. King John, exhausted by his efforts to retain the crown, became ill on 9 October 1216, while journeying in the Fenlands. His baggage train with all his treasure was lost in the Wash on 12 October, and on the 18th the king died. An immediate coronation was essential. The obvious heir was King John's son Henry, but he was a boy of nine, and ambitious Louis was waiting with his men. Henry and his mother Isabella of Angoulême were at Gloucester. There was no time to journey to Westminster Abbey, which in any case was temporarily commandeered by Louis. There were no regalia to hand, but all difficulties were spurned. Henry III was

crowned with his mother's bracelet by
the Bishop of Winchester in Gloucester
Abbey on the feast of St Simon and
St Jude, 28 October 1116, a mere ten
days after King John's death. (Nowa-
days it takes a year to prepare for a
coronation!) One of England's greatest
reigns had begun.

Henry III held a parliament in Gloucester; he was here again in 1241,
consecrating the Bishop of Durham
and receiving the homage of David Ap
Llewellyn, Prince of North Wales. In
1249 the king appointed Master John
of Gloucester 'King's Mason' and in
1250 Master John moved to London
to begin work on Henry's new Westminster Abbey, the church which has
been England's glory ever since. In
1278 Edward I held a parliament here,
when the 'Statutes of Gloucester' were
passed.

One of the most significant royal
events soon followed. In 1306 John
Thokey became Abbot of Gloucester,
and the following year Edward II, aged
23, became King of England. Edward
soon proved to be an inadequate king.
His many failures culminated in his
defeat at Bannockburn in 1314 followed
by years of civil war, and the total
alienation of his queen, Isabella. In
1319 Edward II was feasting with
Thokey in the Abbot's lodging, completed three years before. Observing
the pictures of his predecessors there,
Edward jokingly asked if his own was
among them. The abbot, in something
of a prophetic spirit, answered that he
hoped he should have the king in a
more honourable place. This prophecy
was fulfilled in 1327. Edward was
captured by his enemies in 1326 and
forced to abdicate in favour of his son,

who became King Edward III in 1327. Edward II was taken, a prisoner, to Berkeley Castle, on the way spending Palm Sunday, 5 April, at Gloucester and staying the night at Llanthony Abbey. Popular sympathy wavered between Edward and Isabella, his feared and hated queen. Finally she decided her safety depended on his death. Murderers were sent to the castle. One night hideous shrieks told town and castle of his doom, and drove many to their knees to pray for his soul. His murderers had thrust a red hot poker into his bowels, concealing exterior traces of wounds, to give the impression that he had died a natural death. For a month the body remained at Berkeley. It is said that the abbots of Bristol, Kingswood and Malmesbury refused it burial for fear of Isabella and her paramour Mortimer. But John Thokey arrayed his chariot and horses with magnificent trappings of mourning. He adorned the chariot with the abbey arms and drove the king's body, via Standish, to Gloucester. The Bishop of Llandaff guarded it there for 59 days until the funeral. The king's painter delineated golden lions on the hearse, and other works of art included a wooden image of Edward with a copper-gilt crown. A silver vase was also made to contain the king's heart. On 20 December 1327 a magnificent procession entered Gloucester Abbey for the funeral. The king's many mourners included his murderous widow Isabella, her 15-year old son King Edward III and Mortimer.

To medieval folk, to be murdered came near to being martyred. The dead king soon came to be regarded as a saint, his tomb a martyr's shrine. In three years Edward III had imprisoned

*

Isabella, sent Mortimer to the scaffold and planned a tomb of unsurpassed beauty for his father. In order to provide it with worthy surroundings, the transepts and presbytery of the abbey were transformed by a veil of work in the new architectural style, a most important phenomenon in English art in which the king and his royal masons clearly took personal interest. Truly English, this style, the 'Perpendicular', has spread all over England but never beyond it.

Kings were frequently here in the years that followed. Richard II held parliament here in 1378 in the great hall of the abbey, during which time he and his court so packed the house that the monks had to eat in their dormitory. The House of Lords sat in the guest hall, the Commons in the chapter house, business was transacted in the refectory, and the turf in the cloister was so trampled by wrestling and ball playing that soon no grass was to be seen there. Henry IV held parliament here in 1407, and Henry V in 1420. In 1483, it is said, Richard Duke of Gloucester, who was crowned King Richard III on 6 July, sent instructions from Gloucester to London for the murder of the princes in the Tower that same month.

Henry VIII and Anne Boleyn are said to have stayed a night in the Prior's Lodge in 1535, sleeping in the Henry Room thus named in memory of the event.

Continued on page 15

ABOVE: *The House of the Tailor of Gloucester (9 College Court), immortalized by Beatrix Potter and owned by her publishers. A Gloucester tailor, John Pritchard, was making a coat and waistcoat for the mayor. Returning to his shop after a weekend, he found them mysteriously completed. Beatrix, staying nearby in about 1897, was inspired by this story* to write The Tailor of Gloucester. *A charming exhibit here illustrates the tale, in which mice finish the work.*

FACING PAGE, ABOVE: *The western range of College Green. No. 9 (extreme left) built about 1690. Modillion cornice and pediment; fine staircase. Nos. 11-13, 17th and 18th century. No. 14 (right), 15th-century timber-framed house, for-merly the monastic Almoner's Lodging, with interior evidence of a window for distribution of food.*

FACING PAGE, BELOW: *The southern range of College Green. No. 7 (left) was the monastic granary; 'Tudor' frontage is of 1890. No. 8 (right) has an 18th-century front built on to the remains of a 15th-century timber-framed hall.*

The Dissolution of the Abbey

The greatest change in the life of St Peter's since its foundation in 681 was soon to follow. The abbey surrendered to the king in 1539. On 3 September 1541 the king ordained that it become a cathedral, dedicated to the Holy Trinity. It was to be governed by 37 statutes which provided, among other things, for eight choristers, two schoolmasters, singing men, choir music and a common table, i.e. the members of the college were to dine together as in the monastic days. All this was accomplished some years before the Reformation.

The dissolution of the abbey and the founding of the bishopric did not mean total severance from the past. John Wakeman, the last Abbot of Tewkesbury, and a chaplain to King Henry VIII, became the first bishop in 1541. John Hooper, bishop in 1550, had been a monk of Cleeve Abbey; he became an advocate of the Reformation, a Lutheran and an opponent of churchmen like Bishop Bonner of London and Gardiner of Winchester. Under Mary Tudor, Hooper was imprisoned, then sent back to Gloucester. He was burnt on 9 February 1555 on the site in St Mary's Square which is now occupied by Thornhill's monument to him erected in 1862. Bishop Hooper's timber-framed lodging, dating from about 1500, with a similar but later house next to it, in Westgate Street, is today being used as the Folk Museum. Later bishops of Gloucester include Miles Smith, bishop from 1612 to 1624, a translator of the authorized version of the Bible, and William Warburton, editor of Alexander Pope's works. Deans of Gloucester include William Jennings, last prior of St Oswald's who became the first dean in 1541, and William Laud, dean from 1616 to 1621, a staunch Anglican who strove for loyalty to the Book of Common Prayer and whose love for seemliness is recalled in his communion rails now in the cathedral Lady Chapel. However, his despotic attitude, reflecting that of Charles I, under whom he became Archbishop of Canterbury in 1633, led him to the scaffold on 10 January 1645. A happier dean was William Brough, from 1644 to 1671, under whom, at the restoration of Charles II, the glory of worship and music returned to the cathedral, and its splendid organ case was built during the years 1663 to 1665. Happier, also, than Bishop Hooper was Dean Tucker, 1758 to 1799, who was 'burnt' at Bristol, but only in effigy by foolish critics of his views on economics.

The Monks in Gloucester

The first monks formed communities in a desire to withdraw to solitary places for prayer and to think about life's ultimate values. Many Christians and members of other faiths have wanted to do this. In the 5th century St Benedict played a part of fundamental importance for Christianity by drawing up a Rule by which monks might live, worship and serve the world together in monasteries. Benedictine monks are still governed by this Rule. Women were similarly organized and occupied in nunneries. As time passed, the need for simpler modes of monastic life was met by forming new orders such as the Cistercians (who came to England in 1128), the Cluniacs (who came in 1077) and the Augustinian canons. In medieval Gloucester the monastic orders were represented by the Benedictines in St Peter's and also by the Augustinian canons of Llanthony and St Oswald's. Prinknash Abbey in the woods south-east of Gloucester maintains the Benedictine life today.

There are many reminders of the work of the Benedictines in the partly ruined monastic buildings round Gloucester Cathedral. There is the church where they worshipped, the library where they studied, the cloisters where they taught all who wished to learn and the scriptorium where they reproduced books by hand-writing them before the introduction of printing; and there is the refectory where they ate, the guest house where they gave travellers lodging when it was unsafe

★

FACING PAGE: *Miller's Green, where the monastery vineyard was, and the mill worked by a tributary of the River Twyver, now flowing underneath. To the right Parliament Room, once the main hall of the Abbey; 15th-century on a 13th-century undercroft converted into a visitors' refectory in 1980.*

ABOVE RIGHT: *St John's Church, east front to Northgate Street. The church (except the 14th-century west tower) dates from 1732-4, the work of Edward and Thomas Woodward of Chipping Campden. The top of the spire has been rebuilt on the grass near the modern church hall and cloister.*

RIGHT: *The Deanery, Miller's Green, built c.1730. Fine brick front. Pedimented stone doorway, c.1770. Good staircase and panelling. Regency balconies and gazebo at the back.*

but capable of restoration. The fine 13th-century church, partly preserved by being converted into a mansion at the dissolution of the monasteries (and recently restored by The Department of the Environment) had a large aisled nave for preaching, and a quire. The friars' private chapel is preserved in part. The 13th-century timber roofs are most interesting. In the 14th century a transept was contrived.

A few yards east, across Southgate Street, is Greyfriars, the Franciscan house founded in 1230; its church, ruined but well restored, was rebuilt early in the 16th century and consists of a nave and north aisle of nearly equal width.

The Parish Churches

St John Baptist, Northgate Street, has a 14th-century tower and spire, and an 18th-century classical nave. The pulpit was preached in by George Whitefield, born in Gloucester in 1714, and by John Wesley. The medieval chest, 18th-century reredos, communion rails and mace rests, the monuments and communion plate of 1659 are all very interesting.

St Mary de Crypt, Southgate Street, is cruciform and has Norman work in the crypt and a re-cut west door. It was largely rebuilt, probably by Henry Dene who was prior of Llanthony from 1461 to 1501, but incorporates earlier work. There is a fine Easter sepulchre, sedilia and piscina, and perpendicular

*

to be out at night, the infirmary where they attended the sick and aged, and the almonry where they helped the poor and needy. The monastic orders were of crucial importance for the maintenance of civilization. They preserved the literary and artistic treasures of the past through the Dark Ages; and they maintained a universal 'welfare state' through voluntary service based on love of God and of people. Their destruction at the hands of plundering rulers was incalculably disastrous. Among the services St Peter's Abbey rendered to the cause of learning was the foundation in 1283 of Gloucester College, Oxford, originally for 13 monks from Gloucester. In 1560 it was renamed Gloucester Hall, and then in 1714 it was re-endowed by Worcester Cathedral and renamed Worcester College. Finally, a monk of Gloucester, John Twining, built the New Inn in Northgate Street in about 1450 to accommodate pilgrims to Edward IIs shrine.

The Friars in Gloucester

Friars became established during the 13th century; like monks they took vows of poverty, obedience and chastity, but they were not confined to monasteries. They mingled with the people, preaching and teaching, living in the priories and owning nothing. The orders included the Dominicans or Black Friars, noted for their preaching; the Franciscans or Grey Friars; and the Carmelites or White Friars.

The Blackfriars in Ladybellegate Street, Gloucester, was founded in 1239 and has a cloister surrounded by the usual monastic buildings, including an unusual 'study dormitory' above the South Walk. It is now largely ruinous

stone screens between chancel and chapels with openings whose arches continue upwards to form piers supporting arches. The fine central tower with a lierne rib vault, has, sadly, lost its pinnacles. The Georgian mace rest is interesting. Notable monuments include that of Robert Raikes, whose foundation in Gloucester of the Sunday School movement in 1780 was an act of international importance in the history of the Church and of primary education. There are also brasses, dating from 1544, of John and Joan Cooke, founders of the Crypt Grammar School whose original building of 1539 adjoins the church. George Whitefield was educated here and also at the cathedral King's School.

St Mary de Lode, in St Mary's Square, is cruciform with a central tower. The western tower arch is Norman, the eastern one 13th century, as is the vaulted chancel. The nave is 19th

century. Recent excavations have revealed interesting Roman works.

St Michael, at the Cross (the site of the Roman cross-roads at the city centre). Only the tower of 1465 with a lierne rib vault survives; the rest was demolished in 1956.

St Nicholas, Westgate Street, has a fine perpendicular tower, 'engaged', i.e. with the side aisles extended each side of it; and it has a lierne rib vault. In 1783 the top of the spire was removed and replaced with a coronet and pinnacles. There is a fine Norman south doorway and a tympanum adorned with an *Agnus Dei*. A 14th-century bronze door knocker of the south door exists. There are 'transitional' Norman arcades, fine monuments and an interesting tower clock.

St Margaret's Chapel, London Road, is 13th century and was formerly a leper hospital-chapel.

St Mary Magdalene, London Road,

is 12th century and was once chapel of another leper hospital.

There are also several other memorable churches and chapels of 18th- to 20th-century date.

The Siege of Gloucester

Gloucester suffered badly during the Civil War. It had unexpectedly become 'a Roundhead City' (as Dr Whiting tells us in *Gloucester Besieged*) because of 'Ship Money', – King Charles I's levy to extend his navy – the threat of Virginian tobacco to the local product, the sale of the Forest of Dean to a Roman Catholic and the attitude of Dean Laud, who liked churches to be expensively furnished. Preparations were made for a siege, anticipated because of Gloucester's strategic position. The governor, Colonel Massey, took charge of the city's defence in 1642, lodging in what is now 26 Westgate Street, a fine 16th-century house with a splendid timber-frame elevation visible from the narrow Maverdine Passage. King Charles had his headquarters at Matson House (now Selwyn School) where the initials of his sons, the future Charles II and James II, are scratched on a window. The siege began on 10 August 1643 after the city refused to surrender to the king's army. By 5 September food and gunpowder had run low and a day of fasting and prayer was ordered. On that day, the citizens heard of the approach of parliamentary troops and at last the Royalists withdrew.

Seventeen years of puritanical rule and confusion followed, during which the cathedral was nearly destroyed, its Lady Chapel and little cloister badly damaged, and it was only saved, together with King's and Crypt Schools, by being put in the care of the City Council, whose Mayor still has in consequence a stall in the cathedral quire. Eventually Colonel Massey became a Royalist, and the people, tired of constant hostilities, gladly welcomed the return of a monarchy, and made the Duke of Gloucester Lord High Steward of the city. Permanent scars left behind by this miserable period

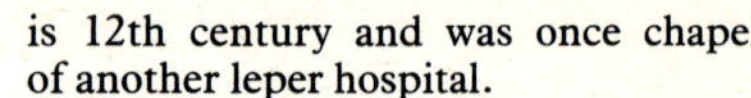

*

LEFT: *A Thames sailing barge in the docks.*

FACING PAGE: *The docks with their 19th-century warehouses. Nearby, in the Customs House in Commercial Road, is the Gloucestershire Regimental Museum.*

include the demolition of the city walls, gates and castle by order of Charles II.

The Port of Gloucester

Queen Elizabeth I granted Gloucester a charter in 1580 declaring it a port. It supplied one ship to the Navy at the time of the Armada in 1588. By 1790 trade had so increased that local merchants began to construct a ship canal to the new docks; this was completed in 1827 by the engineers Robert Mylne and Thomas Telford. Telford also built the fine bridge west of the city at Over. Of the impressive 19th-century brick warehouses round the docks, one is planned by the British Waterways Board to become the National Waterways Museum, and others to contain shops, housing and leisure pursuits.

The Severn Bore is a phenomenon worth witnessing. It consists of a tidal wave produced by the shape of the river and the head of the rising tide meeting the river's downward flow, and may be seen between Newnham and Maisemore about 40 times a year. Another speciality are the eel-like lampreys, a local delicacy.

Gloucester's Industries

Building and allied arts and crafts have been major industries in the service of religion, agriculture, transport and defence in Gloucester from the 7th century onwards. Forest of Dean iron-ore, coal and timber encouraged black-smiths and other iron workers to de-velop their skills. Bell-founding was long a major industry in Gloucester; the recently discovered 'itinerant founder's' furnace and bell-mould in St Oswald's

has already been noted. Hugh the bell-founder appears as a burgess in 1270, and the seal of Sandre, a Gloucester bell-founder of about 1300, was found in the Thames in 1850. John of Glou-cester cast bells for Ely Cathedral in 1346 and Robert Hendley cast many bells here, too, during the latter half of the 15th century. In 1527 Thomas Loveday repaired the mechanism which played the plainsong tunes on the abbey bells. Since their restoration in 1979 these tunes can be heard once again. The founder of three-ton 'Great Peter' in the abbey in 1450 has not been identified. The famous Gloucester bell-founding family of Rudhall began with Abraham who was casting bells from 1689 to 1718; he died in 1735 and is commemorated by a monument in Gloucester Cathedral. The family busi-ness continued until 1829 when it was bought by the Whitechapel Bell-foundry,

London, which today sends bells all over the world. So ended Gloucester's long tradition of bell-founding.

The railways came early to Gloucestershire. In 1839 Isambard Kingdom Brunel became the engineer of a line from Bristol to Gloucester. In the 1840s its gauge was changed from the British standard gauge to Brunel's favourite 'broad gauge', 7 feet wide. The Birmingham and Gloucester Railway was standard gauge and the inconvenience of having to transfer at Gloucester from one gauge to the other led to years of controversy, ending only when the lines were converted to the narrow or standard gauge between 1869 and 1892. Railway-coach and wagon manufacturing continued in Gloucester until recently. Pin-making was for long a significant local industry. Engineering, particularly in the manufacture of aircraft, has been most important in the 20th century. Today there is much industrial development of international importance in Gloucester.

A Tour of 17th- to 19th-Century Gloucester

A detailed description of the buildings of this comparatively modern period integrated into work of the previous 1500 years is impossible. Here, in a brief tour, are some of the most interesting examples of the period, beginning with College Green to the south and west of the cathedral. We start at the south-east corner of the Green, facing the cathedral, having entered it via College Court, a narrow passage from Westgate Street. The medieval pedestrian entrance was probably used by pilgrims to Edward II's shrine. Number 9 was in 1979 restored as Beatrix Potter's 'House of the Tailor of Gloucester'. The eastern side of the court was demolished in the 1940s to build a multiple store, the wall of which could easily be rebuilt further east and picturesque shop fronts recreated in front of it. Turn left into College Green for a rapid survey of its houses, most of which were rebuilt in the 17th to 19th centuries on the sites of monastic buildings. Passing numbers 1 to 4, King Edward's Tower is all that remains of the gate built by Edward I. Number 6 is the sexton's house rebuilt in the 17th century; 7 was originally the monastic granary; 8 was probably a monastic timbered guest hall, now with a Georgian front; 9, a fine house of 1690, was another monastic building converted; and 14, next

ABOVE: *Ladybellegate House, corner of Ladybellegate and Longsmith Street. Early 18th century with elaborate Rococo plasterwork inside. This was the town house of the Guise family of Elmore. The family of Robert Raikes, who in 1780 founded the Sunday School movement, at one time lived here.*

LEFT: *18th-century Rococo plasterwork ceiling in the front hall of Ladybellegate House.*

FACING PAGE: *Hare Lane. This 16th-century building is popularly called the 'Raven Tavern', and once belonged to the Hoare family, members of which emigrated to America. It was restored in 1950 and is now an old people's club. The 'Old Fish Shop' nearby was built about 1535.*

to the Norman St Mary's Gate, was the monastic almonry. Through the second arch on our right we enter Miller's Green; on its left is number 1, the Deanery, of about 1730, with gate piers and pedimented doorway of about 1770; 2 is on the site of the monastic water mill, originally worked by the river Twyver which now flows through a culvert; number 3, a few yards ahead on the right of the narrow road is of the 17th century; and on the left is the Abbot's Lodging. Continuing clockwise round Miller's Green is Parliament Room and number 7 is traditionally the organist's house.

From Miller's Green one may go west through St Mary's Gate into St Mary's Square where St Mary de Lode is to be found, also to Archdeacon Street for St Oswald's, or east, past number 3 (see above), the Little Cloister and abbey infirmary arches with the old Bishop's Palace (former Abbot's Lodging) north of the nearby wall, to Dulverton House within which is evidence of a medieval building. From here go round the east end of the cathedral and out through either the Via Sacra gate, opened in 1977, to Northgate Street or on past 16th-century King's School House and late-17th-

century Wardle House to the south of the cathedral, and via College Court to Westgate Street. This, though ruined in recent years, has several interesting old buildings concealed behind modern fronts. Walking in a westerly direction we pass College Street (leading to the cathedral, with 16th-century buildings and the King Edward's Tower on its west side); St Nicholas House; St Nicholas Church, where on our right is the modern Fountain Square and St Mary's Square, replacing medieval houses; and then 400 yards further on, St Bartholomew's Hospital, built in 1788. Returning towards the city

ABOVE LEFT: *Bearland Lodge, Longsmith Street. An early 18th-century house, with a modillion cornice and pediment with figures carved in high relief by John Ricketts.*

BACK COVER: *Miller's Green from the back. Left, Little Cloister House in which was the Misericord where the monks could eat meat. In the foreground is the lawn of the old Bishops' Palace, now King's School.*

Lane nearby, and then on via Westgate Street where the Fleece Hotel has a 12th-century vaulted underground room to College Court, from which this suggested tour of the city began.

Music and Gloucester

Americans will be interested to read that the tune of their national anthem was written by a Gloucester boy, John Stafford Smith, who was born in 1750 son of the cathedral organist. From Gloucester he went to London, becoming a chorister and later organist of the Chapel Royal and lay vicar of Westminster Abbey. He wrote many songs, one of which, 'Anacreon', was the one to become so popular in America.

The Three Choirs Festival, shared by the cathedral choirs of Gloucester, Worcester and Hereford, is the oldest annual musical festival with a continuous history, in the world. The festival takes place in Gloucester every three years and in Worcester and Hereford in the intervening years. The 250th festival was celebrated at Gloucester in 1977. Its beginning was stimulated by the annual Festival of the Corporation of the Sons of the Clergy in St Paul's, London, from 1678 onwards. From the first it had two objectives, which have been pursued until the present day – financial assistance to the widows and orphans of the clergy and a meeting for those interested in choral music. Its repertoire includes the leading soloists and orchestras of England, as well as the three cathedral organists and choirs. Such choirs are in England statutory parts of each cathedral body. Their activities are as old as Christianity and indeed derive from Jewish worship centuries before Christ. Today their music is appreciated more widely than ever before and attracts vast numbers of people from all over the world.

centre by the south side of Westgate we pass Bishop Hooper's lodging, Quay Street, leading to the prison, rebuilt in 1790, to Berkeley Street where we can turn right on to the Via Sacra.

The Via Sacra is a walkway or city trail marked by dark paving stones and passes most of the city's historic buildings. It takes us, via the 17th-century Fountain Inn, left into Longsmith Street, past 18th-century Bearland House, Bearland Lodge, Ladybellegate House, former home of the families of Guise and Raikes, and right into Ladybellegate Street. The Gloucestershire Regimental Museum is nearby. It turns left (eastwards) into Blackfriars, across Southgate Street to Greyfriars, on to Constitution Walk, and left again (northwards) following the line of the vanished Roman walls, past the city library and museum, the modern shopping precinct with car park and across Eastgate Street with the remains of the Roman East Gate, recently exposed to view in a gigantic 'glass case' and admirably described. Nearby is the 18th-century building of Sir Thomas Rich's School, founded in 1666 and now in modern buildings in Elmlease. Nearby also are the modern King's Walk, King's Square, railway station, leisure centre and hospital. Alternatively, when in Southgate Street we can go a quarter of a mile south and turn left (eastwards) into Spa Road, where there are some fine houses of about 1820, recalling the former spa. When in Eastgate Street we can turn left towards the Cross (the fine medieval cross was demolished in 1751) at which is the medieval tower of St Michael's, with a bell museum, and from which we can visit the New Inn in Northgate Street, with old buildings in Hare

ACKNOWLEDGMENTS

All the photographs are by David Miller, with the exception of page 1 by Aerofilms Ltd. Map on page ii cover drawn by Robert Clarke.

SBN 85372 329 X